A **Literature Kit™** FOR

Sing Down the Moon

By Scott O'Dell

Written by Michelle Jensen

GRADES 5 - 6

Classroom Complete Press
P.O. Box 19729
San Diego, CA 92159
Tel: 1-800-663-3609 | Fax: 1-800-663-3608
Email: service@classroomcompletepress.com

www.classroomcompletepress.com

ISBN – 13: 978-1-77167-248-1

 We acknowledge the financial support of the Government of Canada through the Book Publishing Industry Development Program (BPIDP) for our publishing activities.

Critical Thinking Skills

Sing Down the Moon

Level	Skills for Critical Thinking	1	2-3	4-6	7-9	10-11	12-13	14-16	17-19	20-21	22-23	Writing Tasks	Graphic Organizers
LEVEL 1 Remembering	• Identify Story Elements	✓	✓	✓	✓	✓	✓	✓	✓	✓	✓	✓	✓
	• Recall Details	✓	✓	✓	✓	✓	✓	✓	✓	✓	✓	✓	✓
	• Match		✓	✓									
	• Sequence Events		✓	✓		✓		✓		✓			
LEVEL 2 Understanding	• Compare & Contrast		✓	✓	✓	✓			✓	✓			✓
	• Summarize			✓	✓	✓		✓			✓	✓	✓
	• State Main Idea	✓		✓			✓			✓			
	• Describe	✓	✓	✓		✓	✓	✓	✓	✓			
	• Classify				✓				✓		✓		
LEVEL 3 Applying	• Plan			✓			✓		✓			✓	✓
	• Interview							✓				✓	
	• Infer Outcomes	✓	✓	✓		✓	✓	✓	✓	✓			
LEVEL 4 Analysing	• Draw Conclusions	✓	✓	✓	✓	✓		✓	✓	✓	✓		
	• Identify Supporting Evidence	✓	✓	✓		✓	✓	✓		✓	✓		✓
	• Motivations	✓	✓	✓	✓	✓			✓		✓		
	• Identify Cause & Effect		✓	✓		✓						✓	
LEVEL 5 Evaluating	• State & Defend An Opinion		✓	✓	✓	✓		✓	✓		✓		
	• Make Judgements	✓	✓				✓	✓		✓	✓		✓
LEVEL 6 Creating	• Predict	✓	✓	✓	✓	✓		✓	✓	✓	✓		
	• Design											✓	
	• Create			✓								✓	
	• Imagine Alternatives		✓	✓			✓		✓	✓		✓	

Based on Bloom's Taxonomy

Contents

Assessment Rubric

Sing Down the Moon

Student's Name: ______________________ Assignment: ________________ Level: ________

	Level 1	Level 2	Level 3	Level 4
Comprehension of Novel	Demonstrates a limited understanding of the novel	Demonstrates a basic understanding of the novel	Demonstrates a good understanding of the novel	Demonstrates a thorough understanding of the novel
Content • information and details relevant to focus	Elements incomplete; key details missing	Some elements complete; details missing	All required elements completed; key details contain some description	All required elements completed; enough description for clarity
Style • effective word choice and originality • precise language	Little variety in word choice. Language vague and imprecise	Some variety in word choice. Language somewhat vague and imprecise	Good variety in word choice. Language precise and quite descriptive	Writer's voice is apparent throughout. Excellent choice of words. Precise language
Conventions • spelling, language, capitalization, punctuation	Errors seriously interfere with the writer's purpose	Repeated errors in mechanics and usage	Some errors in convention	Few errors in convention

STRENGTHS:

WEAKNESSES:

NEXT STEPS:

Teacher Guide

Our resource has been created for ease of use by both TEACHERS and STUDENTS alike.

Introduction

Our literature kit is designed to give the teacher a number of helpful ways of making the study of this novel a more enjoyable and profitable experience for the students. Our guide features a number of useful and flexible components, from which the teacher can choose. It is not expected that all of the activities will be completed.

One advantage to this approach to the study of a novel is that the student can work at his or her own speed, and the teacher can assign activities that match the student's abilities.

Our literature kit divides the novel by chapters and features reading comprehension and vocabulary questions. Themes include gender roles, equality, cultural assimilation, persecution, racism, internment, wars and even genocide. Sing Down the Moon gives classrooms a chance to discuss the importance of understanding the world view of others and the importance of not judging other cultures.

How Is Our Literature Kit™ Organized?

STUDENT HANDOUTS

Chapter Activities *(in the form of reproducible worksheets)* make up the majority of this resource. For each group of chapters, there are BEFORE YOU READ activities and AFTER YOU READ activities.

- The BEFORE YOU READ activities prepare students for reading by setting a purpose for reading. They stimulate background knowledge and experience, and guide students to make connections between what they know and what they will learn. Important concepts and vocabulary from the chapter(s) are also presented.

- The AFTER YOU READ activities check students' comprehension and extend their learning. Students are asked to give thoughtful consideration of the text through creative and evaluative short-answer questions and journal prompts.

Six **Writing Tasks** and three **Graphic Organizers** are included to further develop students' critical thinking and writing skills, and analysis of the text. *(See page 6 for suggestions on using the Graphic Organizers.)* The **Assessment Rubric** *(page 4)* is a useful tool for evaluating students' responses to the Writing Tasks and Graphic Organizers.

PICTURE CUES

This resource contains three main types of pages, each with a different purpose and use. A **Picture Cue** at the top of each page shows, at a glance, what the page is for.

Teacher Guide
- Information and tools for the teacher

Student Handout
- Reproducible worksheets and activities

Easy Marking™ Answer Key
- Answers for student activities

EASY MARKING™ ANSWER KEY

Marking students' worksheets is fast and easy with this **Answer Key**. Answers are listed in columns—just line up the column with its corresponding worksheet, as shown, and see how every question matches up with its answer!

Every question matches up with its answer!

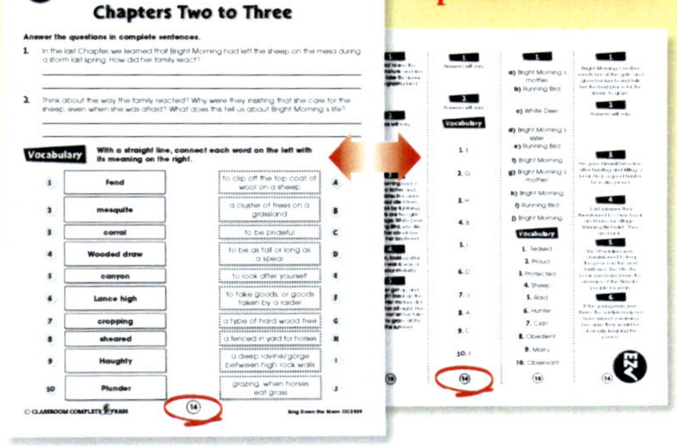

1,2,3
Graphic Organizers

The three **Graphic Organizers** included in this **Literature Kit™** are especially suited to a study of ***Sing Down the Moon***. Below are suggestions for using each organizer in your classroom, or they may also be adapted to suit the individual needs of your students. The organizers can be used on a projection system or interactive whiteboard in teacher-led activities, small group activities, and/or photocopied for use as student worksheets. To evaluate students' responses to any of the organizers,you may wish to use the **Assessment Rubric** *(on page 4)*.

PLOT SUMMARY

Use the graphic organizer to gather facts and quotes on the plot. Students identify the event that starts the conflict or struggle in the story. Find the main events that cause the conflict to rise, and finally reach the climax. Then, finish off with the conclusion. Students are encouraged to use quotes from the text to describe the rising and falling action.
Found on Page 53.

BOTH SIDES OF THE STORY

Students will look at the same event in the story from two perspectives. For example, when the 'Long Knives' tell Old Bear that he needs to keep the peace. Students can understand the need for the American soldiers to stop the fighting among Native nations and between the Americans and the Navaho. Can they understand the justification to continue the fighting and the raids? This graphic organizer will help students gather facts and quotes to try to present two sides to any story situation.
Found on Page 54.

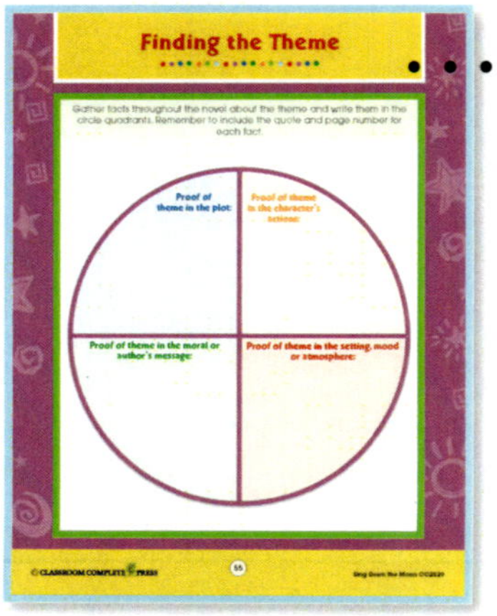

FINDING THE THEME

Students will gather information throughout the text in order to understand one of the Themes as it is presented in the novel. Understanding the plot, character development, mood, and author's message is essential for understanding the theme. Students use the quadrants of the circle to gather facts and quotes. Students record the quote and page number. At the end of the book, students will have organized facts and quotes ready to help them write an analysis of a Theme for the novel.
Found on Page 55.

Bloom's Taxonomy* for Reading Comprehension

The activities in this resource engage and build the full range of thinking skills that are essential for students' reading comprehension. Based on the six levels of thinking in Bloom's Taxonomy, questions are given that challenge students to not only recall what they have read, but to move beyond this to understand the text through higher-order thinking. By using higher-order skills of applying, analyzing, evaluating and creating, students become active readers, drawing more meaning from the text, and applying and extending their learning in more sophisticated ways.

This **Literature Kit™**, therefore, is an effective tool for any Language Arts program. Whether it is used in whole or in part, or adapted to meet individual student needs, this resource provides teachers with the important questions to ask, inspiring students' interest and creativity, and promoting meaningful learning.

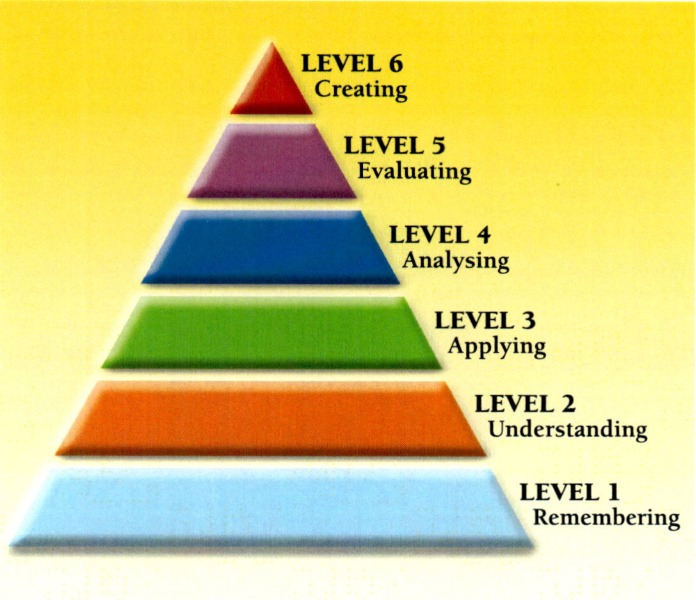

BLOOM'S TAXONOMY: 6 LEVELS OF THINKING

**Bloom's Taxonomy is a widely used tool by educators for classifying learning objectives, and is based on the work of Benjamin Bloom.*

Teaching Strategies

WHOLE-CLASS, SMALL GROUP AND INDEPENDENT STUDY

This study guide contains the following activities:

Before Reading Activities: themes are introduced and thought-provoking questions put forward for the students to consider.

Vocabulary Activities: new and unfamiliar words are introduced and reviewed.

After Reading Questions: the first part of this section includes short answer questions dealing with the content of the text. The second part features questions that are more open-ended and feature concepts from the higher order of Bloom's Taxonomy.

Writing Tasks: creative writing assignments based on Bloom's Taxonomy that relate to the plot of the particular chapters.

A comprehension quiz is also included comprised of multiple-choice, true/false and short-answer questions.

Graphic Organizers: three full-page reproducible sheets have been included and can be used for teaching purposes throughout the text.

Bonus Sheets are also available online.

The study guide can be used in a variety of ways in the classroom depending on the needs of the students and teacher: The teacher may choose to use an independent reading approach with students capable of working independently. It also works well with small groups, with most of the lessons being quite easy to follow. Finally, in other situations, teachers will choose to use it with their entire class.

Teachers may wish to have their students keep a daily reading log so that they might record their daily progress and reflections.

Summary of the Story

Sing Down the Moon *is a story told by a young Navaho woman. At the beginning, we meet Bright Morning, the central character. The reader also learns about her connection to the land and the environment. It is spring and she feels mature and hopeful. She takes her family's sheep to the grazing grounds. Unfortunately, she is captured and sold into slavery. However, she does not accept her fate. She escapes with the help of friends, and returns home. Sadly, her husband-to-be is badly injured in the escape. When they arrive home, they find that things are not as they once were. When the army forces them out of their canyon, they begin the long walk to Fort Sumner. In the end, Bright Morning sees the relocation as the end of her people. She cannot accept the loss of her culture, so once again she plans to escape. She leads her young family away, back to their home in the Chelly Canyon.*

The book is well-researched and includes historically-accurate details of the life of the Navaho people from Chelly Canyon. Woven into the story is: the Navaho traditional hunter-gather lifestyle, the coming-of-age ceremony, the dangers of Spanish slavers, and the tragic Long Walk forced upon the Navaho people in the mid-1800s.

Suggestions for Further Reading

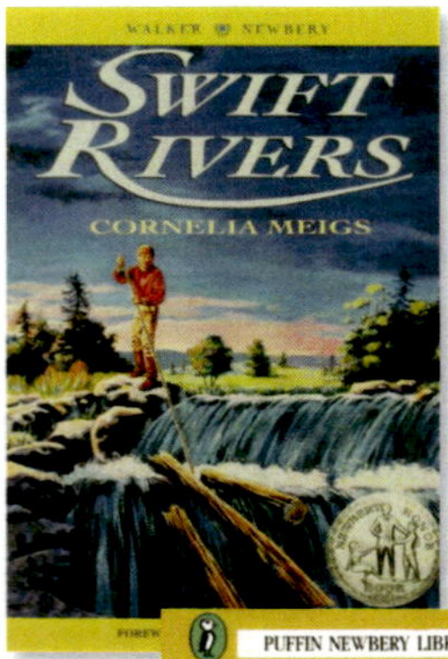

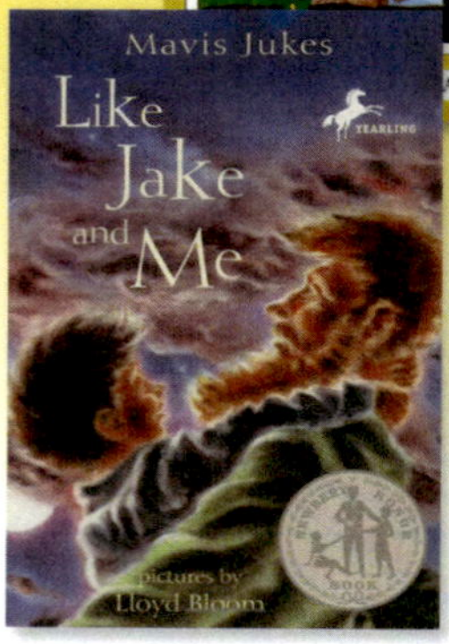

OTHER BOOKS BY SCOTT O'DELL

Island of the Blue Dolphins © 1960

The King's Fifth © 1966

The Black Pearl © 1967

Zia © 1976

Sarah Bishop © 1980

Black Star, Bright Dawn © 1988

My Name is Not Angelica © 1989

OTHER RECOMMENDED RESOURCES

Cornelia Meigs, ***Swift Rivers*** © 1932

Eloise Jarvis McGraw, ***Moccasin Trail*** © 1952

Meindert De Jong, ***Shadrach*** © 1953

Dorothy Rhoads, ***The Corn Grows Ripe*** © 1956

Robert Lawson, ***The Great Wheel*** © 1957

William O. Steele, ***The Perilous Road***© 1958

Kathryn Lasky, ***Sugaring Time*** © 1983

Mavis Jukes, ***Like Jake and Me*** © 1984

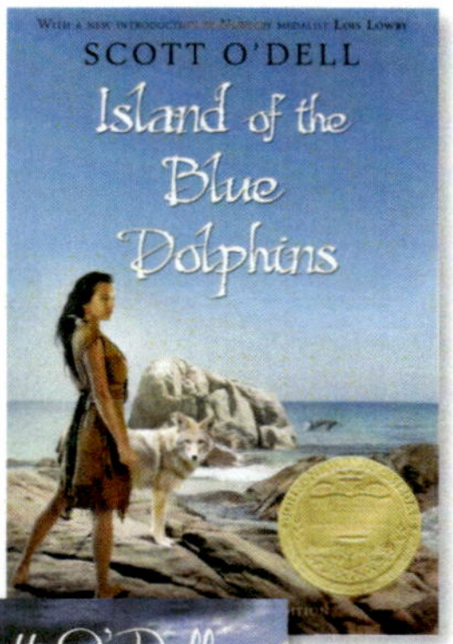

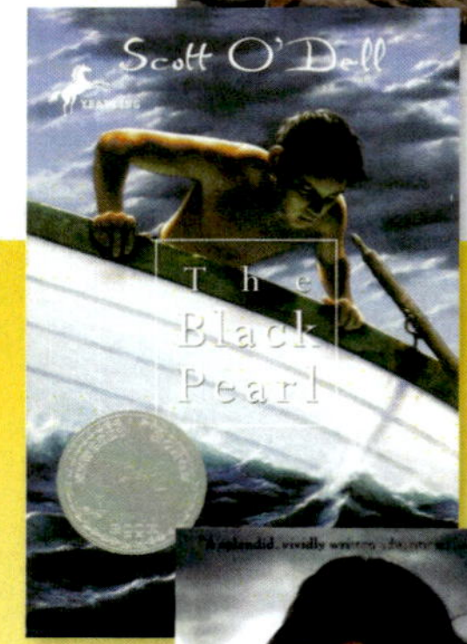

List of Vocabulary

CHAPTER 1
• mesa • greening • barrancas • flock • aspen grove • pinon

CHAPTERS 2 TO 3
• fend • mesquite • corral • wooded draw • canyon • lance high • cropping • obedient • sheared • goading • Utes • astride • haughty • Hogan • plunder • foolhardy

CHAPTERS 4 TO 6
• Hogan • slavers • thong • halt • pine • hobble • Jicarilla Apache • blood brothers • Nez Percé

CHAPTERS 7 TO 9
• rafters • camisa • surly • disposition • pigeon-toed • Zuni • haggle • adobe • churring • omen • velveteen • steal away • baile • cloaks • fiesta • slain • cunning • vengeful • boughs • tortillas • Penitentes • hobbled • bridles • pintos • tethered • grove

CHAPTERS 10 TO 11
• scornfully • crest • ridge • a draw • reins • ravine • neigh • solemnly • lances • dusk • leagues

CHAPTERS 12 TO 13
• litter • sycamore • gaunt • mottled berries • shorn • womanhood ceremony • Kin-nadl-dah • industrious • obedient • comely • yucca root • floundered • taunted

CHAPTERS 14 TO 16
• pinto beans • tending • abandoned • hatchets • spurred • lean-to • tethered • crevice • broth • feat • bore • clans • captivity

CHAPTERS 17 TO 19
• portals • prodded • league • trudged • falter • jeer • waned • lame • crone • carrying board • straggling • ragged • buzzards • fleecy • coyote • brush • quarrelsome • headmen • hides • idle • slain

CHAPTERS 20 TO 21
• buttress • gruel • scold • tend • waning • gourd • forsaken • spindly

CHAPTERS 22 TO 23
• gaunt • haunches • dozes • ramparts • crimson • shorn • gnarled

Spotlight On...

Scott O'Dell

Scott O'Dell was born May 23, 1898 in Los Angeles, California. His real name was O'Dell Gabriel Scott, but a clerical error switched his name around to Scott O'Dell. He liked the sound of his new name, so he had it legally changed.

O'Dell had many jobs in his long life: soldier, farmer, script-reader, set-builder, and camera man for Paramount studios. He worked on many big films from the 1920s, and often spoke of his one claim-to-fame in the film industry: his hands were used for a scene in "The Sheik" with Rudolph Valentino.

He was the author of many adult books, which often developed from his interest in strong and unique individuals. He wrote historical fiction to bring to life the interesting people he had researched. While researching for his books, he and his wife would travel to the locations. Much of Scott O'Dell's writing shows a clear narrative style. Common themes include the human spirit's triumph over adversity, the strength of women, and the struggle for justice. Scott O'Dell said in an interview in 1984 with Conrad Wesselhoeft: "The only reason I write is to say something. I've forsaken adults because they're not going to change, though they may try awfully hard. But children can and do change."

Did You Know?

- **Scott O'Dell served in the Army in World War I, then the Air Force and Coast Guard Auxiliary in World War II.**
- **Scott O'Dell had originally written the novel *Island of the Blue Dolphins* as an adult book, but his publisher recognized the book's value for young people, and Scott O'Dell's career as a children's author was born.**
- **His final novel, *Thunder Rolling in the Mountains*, was finished by his wife Elizabeth Hall after Scott O'Dell died in 1989.**

NAME: ______________________________

Chapter One

Answer the questions in complete sentences.

1. What do people say will bring good luck? Or bad luck? Do they affect the way you behave?

____

____

2. What do you know about the Navaho people?

____

____

Vocabulary

Complete each sentence with a word from the list.

aspen	**corral**	**greening**	**mesa**
barrancas	**flock**	**grove**	**pinon**

1. A deep ravine or gorge or cliffs is called a ______________.

2. A large high land, with a flat top and steep sides is called a ______________.

3. A group of sheep is called a herd or a ______________.

4. A stand of trees all of the same kind is called a ______________.

5. An enclosed place to keep livestock—like horses or sheep—is called a ______________.

6. When spring comes, trees often change from bare and dead looking plants, to vibrant budding trees. This process can be called ______________ because of the change in color of all the plants.

7. The ______________ tree is a deciduous, leaf bearing tree.

8. The ______________ tree is a coniferous tree, bearing needles and edible seeds .

After You Read

NAME: ____________________

Chapter One

1. Put a check mark (✓) next to the answer that is most correct.

a) Who is telling the story?

- ◯ **A** An old man.
- ◯ **B** A young man.
- ◯ **C** An old woman.
- ◯ **D** A young woman.

b) Why is the narrator excited for Spring?

- ◯ **A** All the world was turning green.
- ◯ **B** She had another chance to prove that she could care for the sheep.
- ◯ **C** The rain storms would stop, and she was afraid of storms.
- ◯ **D** Her mother would talk to her again.

c) Who did the sheep belong to?

- ◯ **A** The narrator's mother.
- ◯ **B** Lapana, her sister.
- ◯ **C** Her brother.
- ◯ **D** All the women of the tribe.

2. Answer each question with the correct word(s) from the Chapter.

a) The Navaho people relied on farming and hunting for their food. From Chapter one, what are two foods that they grew to eat?

b) Based on this Chapter, what animals did they hunt?

c) What animals did they raise?

d) What are 3 types of trees mentioned in this Chapter?

e) What is the name of the Spring month for the narrator?

Chapter One

Answer each question with a complete sentence.

1. Explain 2 reasons why Bright Morning was so excited to see the early Spring rains.

2. Find 2 quotes that give us a hint of the spiritual beliefs in Bright Morning's culture.

3. Describe Bright Morning's family and friends.

4. Why is it so important for Bright Morning to take the sheep back up to the grazing lands?

5. Last Spring, how did Bright Morning's mother teach her the importance of caring for the sheep? (3 details)

Journaling Prompt

Bright Morning is excited to get outside and enjoy the Spring day. Do you have a favorite season or time of year? Take a moment to describe your favorite time of year. Describe what you can see, hear, smell, taste, touch, think about and why it is your favorite time of year.

Before You Read

NAME: ______________________

Chapters Two to Three

Answer the questions in complete sentences.

1. In the last Chapter, we learned that Bright Morning had left the sheep on the mesa during a storm last spring. How did her family react?

____

____

2. Think about the way the family reacted. Why were they insisting that she care for the sheep, even when she was afraid? What does this tell us about Bright Morning's life?

____

____

Vocabulary

With a straight line, connect each word on the left with its meaning on the right.

1	**fend**	to clip off the top coat of wool on a sheep	A
2	**mesquite**	a cluster of trees on a grassland	B
3	**corral**	to be prideful	C
4	**wooded draw**	to be as tall or long as a spear	D
5	**canyon**	to look after yourself	E
6	**lance high**	to take goods, or goods taken by a raider	F
7	**cropping**	a type of hard wood tree	G
8	**sheared**	a fenced in yard for horses	H
9	**haughty**	a deep ravine/gorge between high rock walls	I
10	**plunder**	grazing, when horses eat grass	J

Chapters Two to Three

1. Match each quote with the name of the character who said it.

☐ **a)** "The grass is better to the south, beyond the aspen grove."

☐ **b)** "It would be wiser if there was only one of the twins instead of two. There is not enough strength to divide between them."

☐ **c)** "Some poor man may marry her. He will see that she eats little and think it will not matter whether he is poor or not."

☐ **d)** "I eat like a man."

☐ **e)** "More likely he will see that her mother owns many sheep."

☐ **f)** "Three of your sheep have strayed."

☐ **g)** "I hope that he does not kill another bear. If he does he will call himself Very Tall Boy and we will have much trouble with him."

☐ **h)** "For his sake I wished he would kill another bear."

☐ **i)** "Last summer they threatened to come back and burn our village."

☐ **j)** "We have kept the peace."

Vocabulary

Complete each sentence with a word from the list.

clan	**marry**	**observant**	**proud**	**sheep**
hunter	**obedient**	**protected**	**raid**	**teased**

1. The girls ____________ each other about their looks and future husbands.
2. Bright Morning's mother thinks that Tall Boy is too ____________.
3. In Navaho culture, men hunted and ____________ the village.
4. Women farmed and raised ____________.
5. The soldiers wanted the Navaho to keep the peace and not __________other tribes.
6. Tall Boy was a good ____________ and very brave.
7. Old Bear was the elder who spoke for the ____________.
8. Bright Morning would be a good wife because she was strong and ____________.
9. Bright Morning wanted to ____________ Tall Boy.
10. While caring for the sheep, the girls had to be ____________, to watch for dangers.

NAME: ____________________

Chapters Two to Three

Answer each question with a complete sentence.

1. How does Bright morning's mother let her know that she trusts her to take the sheep?

2. What do you think Running Bird meant when she said "it would have been wiser if there was only one of the twins, instead of two." Why do you think she used the word 'wiser'?

3. Bright Morning likes Tall Boy. How did he get his name? What does this tell us about him?

4. Find a quote showing the relationship Bright Morning's clan has with the Long Knives.

5. Why do you think the soldiers wanted to stop the Navaho from raiding other Native Nations? Why did the warriors go to fight the Ute?

6. What do you think would have been the reaction of the 'Long Knives', if the soldiers had found all the young men home, instead of out on a raid?

Journaling Prompt

What jobs or chores do you have to do in your family? What happens if people don't do their chores? What happens if they do? Write about the rights and responsibilities you have in your family.

NAME: ______________________

Before You Read

Chapters Four to Six

Answer the questions in complete sentences.

1. In the previous Chapters, the girls mention that the warriors are going to raid the Utes, indicating that they are enemies. What do you think would cause the Navaho and Utes to be enemies?

____

____

2. What do you think about Bright Morning's quality of life? What would you enjoy? What wouldn't you enjoy?

____

____

Vocabulary

With a straight line, connect each word on the left with its meaning on the right.

1	**hogan**	A Native American Nation from Idaho to Oregon	A
2	**slavers**	stop	B
3	**thong**	an evergreen tree	C
4	**halt**	not related, but sworn to help each other	D
5	**Apache**	Bright Morning's type of house	E
6	**Nez Percé**	tie a horse's front legs together so he can't go far	F
7	**hobble**	A Native American nation from Canada	G
8	**pine**	someone who catches and sells people	H
9	**blood brothers**	a leather cord	I

NAME: ______________________________

Chapters Four to Six

1. Number the events from 1 to 6 in the order they occurred in the Chapter.

☐ **a)** Bright Morning and Running Bird were gagged and tied to the saddle.

☐ **b)** The girls were afraid to see a wolf following them.

☐ **c)** Bright Morning saw a Nez Perce girl who gave her a look that 'chilled' her.

☐ **d)** Bright Morning remembered the girl who had been stolen by slavers.

☐ **e)** They traveled South with the North Star behind them.

☐ **f)** The girls refused to eat, even when threatened with a stick.

2. In the chart, write down the cause or effect for the following causes and effects.

CAUSE	EFFECT
a) The Black Dog barked a warning...	
b)	...Running Bird screamed.
c) Black Dog tried to bite the Spaniard...	
d)	...Bright Morning slept with her arm around Black Dog.
e)	...the girls did not eat even when threatened.
f)	...Bright Morning noticed the Nez Perce girl.

NAME: ______________________________

Chapters Four to Six

Answer each question with a complete sentence.

1. What is the significance of: "Right at the moment Running Bird asked me what my father had said about the soldiers, I jumped up and began to dance."

2. In Chapter 6, Bright Morning says about her black dog: "He would not have left the sheep alone, so I knew that my mother had come to the mesa and driven the flock home." Why is this important to Bright Morning?

3. Based upon what you know so far, what do you think is the main struggle for Bright Morning?

4. Compare and contrast how Bright Morning behaves in these Chapters with that of her friend Running Bird. How are their actions similar? How are they different?

5. What is the plan the girls make for escaping the Slavers? How are they prevented from escaping?

6. What mood does the author set at the end of Chapter 6? Find a quote that shows how the author sets the mood.

Journaling Prompt

All parents try to prepare their children for the dangers they may face. What do your parents warn you about? What do they tell you to do if you are approached by strangers?

Before You Read

NAME: ____________________

Chapters Seven to Nine

Answer the question in a complete sentence.

1. Why do you think Bright Morning followed the Spaniard at the end of Chapter 6? Why didn't she run away or put up a fight?

____

____

2. What do you think Bright Morning will have to do in the home? What do you imagine the living conditions will be like?

____

____

Vocabulary

Write a complete sentence using the following words. Make sure that the meaning of each word is clear in your sentence.

Surly ____

____

Disposition ____

____

Haggle ____

____

Churring ____

____

Cunning ____

____

Boughs ____

____

Hobbled ____

____

Bridles ____

____

Tethered ____

____

NAME: ______________________

Chapters Seven to Nine

1. **Circle T if the statement is TRUE or F if it is FALSE.**

T F a) Bright Morning is taken to a house to be a servant for the wife of a soldier.

T F b) Bright Morning enjoyed the food at the house.

T F c) Bright Morning had to hide her black dog from the lady.

T F d) Rosita is a 12-year-old Navaho girl who likes living with the soldier's family.

T F e) Running Bird is in a house with a Nez Perce girl.

T F f) Bright Morning was warned not to talk to the Nez Perce girl.

T F g) The girls decided to run away on Christmas day.

T F h) Bright Morning had to break the lock to get out of the garden gate.

T F i) They stole 3 horses and rode away during the night.

T F j) A wood cutter helped them get away.

2. **Fill in each blank with the correct word(s) from these Chapters.**

a) Bright Morning showed her resentment to her owner by not ________________ when the Lady told her to walk and smile.

b) The house was owned by a ________________ who was not there often, and his wife.

c) The lady of the house seemed happy that Bright Morning enjoyed learning about ________________ at the church.

d) ________________, the Nez Perce girl had been caught last time she ran away because she didn't have a horse.

After You Read

NAME: ____________________

Chapters Seven to Nine

Answer each question with a complete sentence.

1. Was Rosita happy or lonely living as a slave in the town? Defend your opinion with facts from the story.

____

____

2. How does Bright Morning describe the lady that buys her as a house slave?

____

____

3. What does the lady think about Bright Morning?

____

____

4. Bright Morning becomes homesick for the canyon de Chelly. Compare and contrast her life there and her life in the town. Use facts from the story to support your findings.

____

____

5. Rosita and Bright Morning present two opposite reactions to being enslaved in the town. Why did Rosita adapt to life in the town whereas Bright Morning did not?

____

____

6. Describe the scene in the church ceremony for the Pentinents. List key words that help to create the mood for this scene.

____

____

Journaling Prompt

Bright Morning has been dropped into a whole different way to live. Living in town, she ate different food. She had different chores, different housing and different clothes. She was introduced to a different religion. Have you ever been somewhere that was very different from home? What can you do to adapt to changes? What can you learn from new and different situations?

NAME: ______________________________

Chapters Ten to Eleven

Answer the question in a complete sentence.

1. What precautions were in place to keep Bright Morning from running away?

____

____

2. We don't hear Running Bird's or Nehana's story. What do you think their experience was like?

____

____

Vocabulary

Complete each sentence with a word from the list.

a draw	**dusk**	**leagues**	**ravine**	
crest	**lances**	**neigh**	**ridge**	**scornfully**

1. She crept out in the ____________ when the sun dipped below the horizon.

2. He practices throwing ____________ to be a good warrior and hunter.

3. They looked at her ____________, the anger flashing in their eyes.

4. Bright Morning crept to the ____________ of the hill, and peaked over to watch for the trackers.

5. They traveled many ____________,`til their horses were weary.

6. There was a high rock ____________ that they could hide behind while they rode away.

7. They heard the horse ____________ and knew the trackers were closing in.

8. ____________ is a landform formed by two parallel ridges with low ground in between.

9. The girls climbed out of the ____________ in case the rain caused a flash flood.

After You Read

NAME: ______________________

Chapters Ten to Eleven

1. Fill in each blank with the correct word(s) from these Chapters.

a) The three girls climbed on their stolen pinto horses and headed down towards a small pine __________.

b) The Wood Cutter says that he will lie and tell the trackers that they went the other way, in exchange for a __________.

c) The girls rode the horses in the __________ to hide their tracks.

d) The 3 girls headed __________ because their followers would expect them to go the other direction, straight to their homes.

e) In all, Bright Morning had been captured for about __________ weeks.

f) At __________, the trackers reached the place beside the stream where Nehana had slept.

g) Bright Morning was woken up by __________.

h) Two people came out of the shadows: __________ and his friend Mando.

i) Tall Boy had two weapons: a lance and __________.

j) The Spaniard dropped from his saddle and took a __________ from the holster.

k) Tall Boy and Mando gave a great __________, causing the Spaniard's horse to leap sideways.

l) Bright Morning rode ahead to get the __________.

2. Circle T if the statement is TRUE or F if it is FALSE.

T F **a)** Nehana wanted the horses for revenge, and because the bit and bridle were made of silver and turquoise.

T F **b)** They rode at night, so they had to go slowly.

T F **c)** Once they got out of the river, Bright Morning led them back north toward the canyon de Chelly.

T F **d)** The Spanish slavers said that they wanted the girl's horses, which were stolen.

T F **e)** The leader of the Spanish Slavers was killed by Tall Boy.

NAME: ____________________

Chapters Ten to Eleven

Answer each question with a complete sentence.

1. What do you think were the intentions of the Wood Cutter? What evidence do you base your opinion on?

2. Look back at the dialogue among the girls shortly after running away. Why do you think Nehana wanted to help the other two girls run away?

3. Running Bird was ready to leave Nehana while she slept. Why did Bright Morning disagree?

4. What advantages do the trackers have to catch the girls? What advantages do the girls have to help them escape?

5. Find three facts in these Chapters that prove that Bright Morning really cares for Tall Boy.

6. Does Tall Boy care about Bright Morning? On what do you base this conclusion?

Journaling Prompt

Bright Morning's dog has helped her look after the sheep, warned her when the Spanish slavers approached, kept her company while enslaved, and now barks to identify Tall Boy for her. Do you have a pet? Why or why not? What qualities do you admire or would you admire about your pet? What would be your favorite pet to have? Why?

Before You Read

NAME: ______________________

Chapters Twelve to Thirteen

Answer the questions in complete sentences.

1. Do you think the girls would have escaped without the help of Tall Boy and Mando?

____

____

2. Now that they are back home, do you think life will go on the way it was before Bright Morning and Running Bird were taken by the slavers? Explain why or why not.

____

____

Vocabulary **With a straight line, connect each word on the left with its meaning on the right.**

1	**litter**	cut short	A
2	**sycamore**	pretty	B
3	**shorn**	womanhood ceremony	C
4	**Kin-nadl-dah**	an edible root	D
5	**industrious**	hard worker	E
6	**obedient**	does what they are told	F
7	**comely**	a stretcher	G
8	**floundered**	mocked, jeered	H
9	**taunted**	a tree that loses its leaves seasonally	I
10	**blood yucca**	struggled to adjust	J

Chapters Twelve to Thirteen

1. Put a check mark (✓) next to the answer that is most correct.

a) What did the medicine man use river water and the juice from mottled berries to do?

- ◯ **A** Purify Tall Boy.
- ◯ **B** Make Tall Boy drink.
- ◯ **C** Clean the wound.
- ◯ **D** Paint the ground.

b) What did Bright Morning's sister do to help Tall Boy?

- ◯ **A** Cleaned his wound.
- ◯ **B** Prayed for him.
- ◯ **C** Kept him company.
- ◯ **D** Made his meals.

c) What did Bright Morning's sister really want Bright Morning to understand about Tall Boy's injury?

- ◯ **A** He would never be a good husband.
- ◯ **B** She owed him her life.
- ◯ **C** He needed to change his name again.
- ◯ **D** He would have to learn how to be a medicine man.

d) What was Nehana going to do next?

- ◯ **A** Marry the son of a chief.
- ◯ **B** Return to her home village.
- ◯ **C** Marry Tall Boy.
- ◯ **D** Marry Mando.

e) It was ________'s decision on who Bright Morning would marry.

- ◯ **A** Bright Morning
- ◯ **B** Old Bear, the chief
- ◯ **C** Bright Morning's Mother
- ◯ **D** Bright Morning's Father

After You Read

NAME: ______________________

Chapters Twelve to Thirteen

Answer each question with a complete sentence.

1. Discuss how Bright Morning feels about Tall Boy. Give at least 3 facts from the Chapters to support your answer.

____

____

____

2. How does Bright Morning's mother let her know that she needs to give up on the idea of marrying Tall Boy?

____

____

3. What is the significance of Bright Morning's statement that it was her father's right to decide who she marries, but he always does what his wife wants?

____

____

4. What role did the Men play in the Navaho culture? What would happen to a man who couldn't do what was required of him in the culture? How would he survive? What role would he play?

____

____

5. Why did Tall Boy say: "You think that I went to the white man's village just to rescue you." "You are wrong. I went there for another reason."?

____

____

Journaling Prompt

Have you ever watched TV or met or known someone who was injured in a battle? What do you think it would be like to come home injured from a battle? Think about all the changes that you would have to make in your life when you came home. Soldiers go into service knowing that they could be injured or killed, and yet they go anyway. Reflect on what it would be like to be injured and have to be cared for by others while you try to heal.

NAME: ______________________________

Before You Read

Chapters Fourteen to Sixteen

Answer the questions in complete sentences.

1. Based on what you already know, describe the life of a young girl in a traditional Navaho village in the 1800's.

____

____

2. Describe how important the land and its resources were for Bright Morning and her clan.

____

____

Vocabulary

Complete each sentence with a word from the list.

abandoned	**captivity**	**crevice**	**hatchet**	**tending**
broth	**clans**	**feat**	**pinto beans**	**tethered**

1. The lamb was stuck in a ____________—a crack in the rocks on the cliff.
2. A common meal was corn and ____________.
3. When they were in ____________, Nehana hated being a slave, and tried to run away.
4. The families saw the enemies coming and ____________ the village to hide in the canyon.
5. What a ____________! The boys survived in the wilds with nothing but their spears for two weeks.
6. They ____________ their horses to the post outside the saloon.
7. The women had been in the field ____________ to the sheep.
8. They simmer the bones from the sheep with water from the river to make some ____________ for dinner.
9. Each of the soldiers carried a little axe called a ____________ to cut down the trees.
10. The extended family was called ____________.

NAME: ____________________

Chapters Fourteen to Sixteen

1. Put a check mark (✓) next to the answer that is most correct.

a) Based on the opening paragraph, what season is it?

- ◯ **A** Spring
- ◯ **B** Summer
- ◯ **C** Fall
- ◯ **D** Winter

b) Why doesn't Tall Boy want to run away from the Long Knives?

- ◯ **A** He says they will take their food.
- ◯ **B** He hates the Long Knives and wants to kill them.
- ◯ **C** He likes to fight.
- ◯ **D** He wants to gain back control of the land.

c) How does Bright Morning's father shame Tall Boy?

- ◯ **A** He argues with him.
- ◯ **B** He ignores him.
- ◯ **C** He tells him not to speak.
- ◯ **D** He asks if he could fight with a disabled arm.

d) Why did Tall Boy come up to the mesa?

- ◯ **A** He wanted to help the clans.
- ◯ **B** He wanted to be with Bright Morning.
- ◯ **C** He had injured himself in the climb.
- ◯ **D** He could not keep up with the warriors.

e) How did the people finally know that the soldiers were going to stay in their village?

- ◯ **A** They built a fire pit and stone oven.
- ◯ **B** They trampled all their fields.
- ◯ **C** They burned down their hogans.
- ◯ **D** They cut down all the peach trees.

f) Approximately, how many days did they hide out on the mesa, before leaving to find a new place for their village?

- ◯ **A** 6
- ◯ **B** 10
- ◯ **C** 14
- ◯ **D** 30

NAME: ______________________

Chapters Fourteen to Sixteen

Answer each question with a complete sentence.

1. What is the conflict in this story? What would be the peak or climax of the conflict?

____

____

2. Why does Tall Boy rip the paper up and throw it in the stream?

____

3. During these Chapters, Tall Boy learns something that shakes his sense of identity. What is it? How do you think it will shape his future actions?

____

____

4. In the last Chapter, Bright Morning's sister, mother and Nehana said that they felt sorry for Tall Boy. Does Bright Morning feel sorry for Tall Boy? Explain using facts from these Chapters.

____

____

5. Tall Boy vows to learn to hunt again. Based on what you know of his personality, do you think that he will learn to throw the spear well again? Support your opinion using facts from the story.

____

____

6. What is in a Name? Look at the name of the clans. How do their clan names reinforce the importance of the land to the Aboriginal First Nations?

____

____

Journaling Prompt

The meaning of Names: What is the story behind your name? Find out the meaning of your given name and why you were named that name. What is the origin of your family name? Where does it come from? Did it have a meaning at one time in history other than as a family name? Finally, if you lived during the time of Bright Morning, what name would you give yourself and why?

NAME: ______________________

Chapters Seventeen to Nineteen

Vocabulary

brush
buzzards
carrying board
coyote
crone
falter
fleecy
headmen
hides
idle
jeer
lame
league
portals
prodded
quarrelsome
ragged
slain
straggling
trudged
waned

Across

1. Another word for doors.
3. Birds that eat carrion.
5. To decrease in strength or number.
6. The skins of animals.
7. Fight or argue.
8. To sneer, talk scornfully to someone.
12. Crippled or physically disabled.
13. The wool on a sheep.
14. To struggle to keep up with the group.
15. A derogatory name for an old woman.
16. To walk wearily.
17. To do nothing.

Down

1. To be pushed along.
2. A measure of distance.
3. Low wild scrub grasses and bushes.
4. A baby carrier that allowed a mom to carry a baby on her back.
6. Elders or chiefs who make decisions for the clan.
9. Ripped, torn or patched clothes.
10. A wild dog-like predator.
11. To be unsteady or unsure.
14. To be killed.

NAME: ______________________________

Chapters Seventeen to Nineteen

1. Fill in each blank with the correct word(s) from these Chapters.

a) The opening paragraph in Chapter 17, tells us that a lot of time has gone by because it is now the ________________ season.

b) Bright Morning offers to carry one of the children carried by ________________, a girl her age from the Blue Water Canyon.

c) Tall Boy slipped into the camp. His clothes were torn, and his feet were ________________ and ________________. He ate the mush Bright Morning gave him, but he would not ________________.

d) ________________ is the leader of the clan, now that Old Bear has died. He really couldn't 'lead' since they were forced to go where the soldiers took them. He tried to be optimistic by saying: "Cast your eyes around... You will see many people sitting beside their fires. They are hungry but not ________________. They are cold but they do not ________________. They are unhappy. Yet they are ________________."

e) There were ________________ and coyotes following the Navaho, created by the large number of people who ________________ on the trail.

f) They made it through the hard march and Winter, and started to feel a bit more optimistic, and yet, Bright Morning's Mother ________________ when she saw their new home at Bosque Redondo. She had not cried since they had left their canyon.

g) One of the biggest problems facing Bright Morning's people was ________________. There was nothing to do but gossip and wait and worry. People don't feel good if they are not in control of their lives and doing something purposeful. Most of the men started to accept their fate saying: "The ________________ will tell us what to do. Now they ________________ us. When the time comes they will speak and we will hear them."

After You Read

NAME: ____________________

Chapters Seventeen to Nineteen

Answer each question with a complete sentence.

1. What was Bright Morning's motivation or reason for taking the girl from Little Rainbow?

2. How does her sister react when Little Rainbow can't be found? What is their mother's response?

3. What is the significance of the following statement: "Tall Boy fashioned a carrying board from brush and a piece of cloth."?

4. Compare this Spring to the Spring at the beginning of the novel.

5. Describe the living conditions in their new home.

6. How did the men react to the story of what happened at Sand Creek? How does Bright Morning feel about their reaction?

Journaling Prompt

The last three Chapters are extremely sad. Everyone goes through hardships in their lives, not always as bad as the tragedies described in these last Chapters. What can you do to help someone who is experiencing a hard time? What could you do to help anyone cope with hard times? What—if anything—would help you get through difficult times?

NAME: ______________________

Chapters Twenty to Twenty-One

Answer the questions in complete sentences.

1. How do you think the soldiers will deal with the problems at Fort Sumner?

____

____

____

2. How will the Navaho and Apache respond to the issues they are facing?

____

____

Vocabulary

Choose a word from the list that means the same or nearly the same as the sentence.

buttress	**gourd**	**scold**	**tend**
forsaken	**gruel**	**spindly**	**waning**

☐ **1.** A hard shelled, hollow plant pod, great for storing food and water in it.

☐ **2.** Long and thin and usually weak.

☐ **3.** A thin porridge.

☐ **4.** Abandoned, left behind.

☐ **5.** To tell off.

☐ **6.** A support for a wall.

☐ **7.** To look after.

☐ **8.** To become thinner or smaller in size or power or influence.

NAME: ________________________

Chapters Twenty to Twenty-One

1. Put a check mark (✓) next to the answer that is most correct.

a) Tall Boy's family helps him arrange to marry Bright Morning. How long do negotiations take?

- ◯ **A** a day
- ◯ **B** a week
- ◯ **C** a month
- ◯ **D** a year

b) What does Bright Morning tell Tall Boy that she dreams about?

- ◯ **A** Their Canyon de Chelly.
- ◯ **B** The soldiers attacking and killing them all.
- ◯ **C** Her sheep.
- ◯ **D** The wolves.

c) Why doesn't Tall Boy want to talk about going home?

- ◯ **A** afraid
- ◯ **B** embarrassed
- ◯ **C** depressed
- ◯ **D** ashamed

d) The flour was given out by the soldiers to the ____________ first.

- ◯ **A** Elders
- ◯ **B** Apache
- ◯ **C** Spaniards
- ◯ **D** women and children

e) The soldiers used an Ute man to translate for them. Why was this a problem?

- ◯ **A** The Utes were their traditional enemies.
- ◯ **B** The Utes did not speak Navaho well.
- ◯ **C** The Utes favored the Apache.
- ◯ **D** The Utes were quarrelsome.

NAME: ______________________

Chapters Twenty to Twenty-One

Answer each question with a complete sentence.

1. How and why does Bright Morning's mother change her attitude about Tall Boy?

2. Describe the wedding ceremony. What do you think is the meaning behind the simple actions?

3. Even though she was angry and frustrated with Tall Boy when he said that her sheep were all dead, she doesn't show her anger. Why not?

4. Why is Bright Morning so determined to go back to the village?

5. When Tall Boy is taken away, Bright Morning and her Father go to the fort to get him back. List 3 major cultural misunderstandings between the Navaho and the Long Knives.

Journaling Prompt

Bright Morning is determined, she is self-disciplined and caring. What are your greatest character traits? It's sometimes hard to give ourselves a pat on the back or recognize the good aspects of our own character. If you were at the end of a long and glorious life, what would you want people to recognize about who you were as a person?

Before You Read

NAME: ______________________

Chapters Twenty-Two to Twenty-Three

Answer the questions in complete sentences.

1. Compare the typical wedding today with that of the Navaho in the 1800s. Think about cost, entertainment, church, after church traditions and gift giving. How are they different? How are they the same?

____

____

2. From the very beginning of the book to the very end, Bright Morning brings us into her world that she holds dear. What 3 aspects of her life does she cling to and value, and is determined to get back?

____

____

3. What will Bright Morning do next? Will she wait for her husband, or will she head back home with the supplies she has? Justify your prediction.

____

____

Vocabulary

With a straight line, connect each word on the left with its meaning on the right.

1	**gaunt**	back legs	A
2	**haunches**	bright red	B
3	**dozes**	twisted and knotted	C
4	**ramparts**	high walls like in the outer wall of a castle	D
5	**crimson**	thin and wasted	E
6	**shorn**	a light sleep	F
7	**gnarled**	to cut or shave the wool off a lamb	G

NAME: ______________________________

Chapters Twenty-Two to Twenty-Three

1. Fill in each blank with the correct word(s) from these Chapters.

a) Tall Boy packed their belongings on the ______________ and they left without saying goodbye.

b) They were almost caught while eating just off the trail, by soldiers coming in to the fort driving a small band of ______________ toward the Bosque Redondo.

c) They traveled for ______________ days, and then ran out of flour.

d) Tall Boy took them to a valley called __________, where he had hunted before.

e) There was a pond, and a meadow and many resources. They were able to build a ______________ beside the pond.

f) Bright Morning gave birth to their ______________ in the valley.

g) She was careful not to show too much emotion in case Tall Boy got angry. He said, "We go because I am tired of hearing about ______________."

h) Tall Boy went to scout their old village. He came back to say that there were no soldiers or other Native Americans there. He did admit to seeing an ______________.

i) Once in the canyon, Tall Boy sees a _______, which used to house Navahos a long time ago. He re-carves the hand and foot holds.

j) Black Dog hears something, and Bright Morning finds one of her ewes with a _______.

After You Read

NAME: ______________________

Chapters Twenty-Two to Twenty-Three

Answer each question with a complete sentence.

1. List all the possessions that Bright Morning has accumulated for their move back to their canyon.

____

____

2. What does the comment made by Bright Morning's mother tell us about her thoughts: "He is worse than an old woman. He is like the old men of the Navahos. All of them."?

____

____

3. Throughout the novel, there are social laws that they follow. List some of them. How might another culture cause offense by not knowing the customs of the Navaho?

____

____

____

4. Why do you suppose Tall Boy took Bright Morning to Elk-Running Valley, instead of Canyon de Chelly?

____

____

5. Why does Bright Morning say, "Yet not a day went by that summer or when the snows came that I did not think of my sheep."?

____

____

____

Journaling Prompt

What do you want to do in your future? Do you have a goal or a dream or a certain lifestyle that you want? Describe it in full detail, including how you plan to reach your goal or dream.

Writing Task #1

Chapter 1

Ode to Nature

In the opening scene in the book, Bright Morning describes her world. She felt a joyful connection to her land and her people. Write a poem to a season that you like.

Brainstorm all the words you can think of about a season that you love. Think of different types of words: action words (verbs), descriptors (adverbs, adjectives), people, places, and things (nouns).

Use the words to **write a poem** using the Haiku format. Haiku is a Japanese poem that celebrates nature. Traditionally, Haiku uses 3 lines. The first line has 5 syllables. The second line has 7 syllables. The third line has 5 syllables.

Writing Task #2

Chapter 4

Stranger Danger

In Chapter 4, Bright Morning is captured by a stranger. We still teach children not to talk to strangers. Write a commercial to warn young people about the dangers of talking to strangers. **Follow this action plan:**

- What is the danger?
- What should they do and say when approached by a stranger?
- Who can they go to for help?

Include some catchy music and/or phrases that they could use to remember the lesson. Your commercial could be recorded for either 'radio' or TV. Practice it to make sure that it is polished and professional.

Writing Task #3

Chapters 4 to 6

Interview

Imagine you could travel back in time. Imagine you were transported back to the time this story takes place. Think of 10 questions that you could ask one of the people in these Chapters. You could interview the Spanish slaver, the old woman, or Rosita. After you have asked your questions, think carefully about how the characters are described in these Chapters. Answer the questions the way that you think they would answer them. You may want to do a bit of thinking about why people do what they do. Think about basic needs people have. Think about the conditions for life at the time. Think about peer pressure and prejudice experienced by many groups in history.

Writing Task #4

Chapters 9 to 10

A Graphic Novel

Write a graphic novel.

The topic: escape from slavery for Bright Morning, Running Bird and Nehana. A graphic novel has mostly pictures that show dramatic events in the story.

Pre-Writing: Break the story down to the main events. Take a quote or sentence from the novel for each of the main events. The first event is when Bright Morning is at the church. Nehana signals one more night. The end of the graphic novel is in the end of Chapter 10, when Nehana says, "We go fast and for our lives."

Now draw a dramatic picture for each of the main events. Put the quote or sentence from the book into the page. At this point you may need to add any bridging or transition sentences to help the story flow. Don't add too many though, the story should be mostly key phrases and quotes, letting the pictures tell the rest of the story. Share your graphic novel with your class.

Writing Task # 5

Chapter 16

Tall Boy Character Analysis

1. Gather your facts: What did the character look like, do, like or dislike? How did he behave and interact with others? What were his strengths and weaknesses at the beginning of the story? Remember to gather good quotes to help you prove your point.
2. Note CHANGES: what changed? How? How did he react?
3. Think Like an Author: What role does Tall Boy play in the story? What does he struggle with? Why did the author write him the way he did? Why did the author have him do and say and experience what he experienced in the story?
4. Make a list of how he compares to other main characters in the story.
5. Write a thesis statement: Tall Boy is ________________ in the novel *Sing Down the Moon*.
6. Write an essay including an introductory paragraph, body paragraphs, and a conclusion paragraph.

Writing Task # 6

Chapter 21

Grievance Letter

A grievance letter is a letter that makes a formal complaint. It has 4 parts:

a) Introduces you to the person you are writing.

b) Explains why you have a legitimate complaint.

c) Gives the facts of the situation: What happened? How were you affected? Why does there need to be a change?

d) It finishes with what you want to see done, when you want it done by, and what happens if there is no change.

Write a letter to Abraham Lincoln on behalf of Bright Morning and her people. Write about the loss of their way of life when they were forced off their lands. Be sure to use facts from the novel to include in your grievance letter. Think about what specifically you would like to see done in that time in America's History.

NAME: ______________________________

Word Search Puzzle

Find the following words from the story. The words are written horizontally, vertically, diagonally, and some are written backwards.

antelope	cedar	flock	Nez Perce	stalk
Apache	corn	hogan	pinon	sycamore
aspen	Cottonwood	jay	pinto	Ute
barrancas	crevice	Long Knives	red-tailed hawks	yucca
bean	eagle	mesa	Spaniards	Zuni
bear	elk	mesquite	speckled trout	
canyon	ewes	Navaho	squash	

d	j	y	n	p	a	r	e	i	l	h	f	r	q	n	k	t	n	f	j	d	b	e	q	v
f	u	o	t	c	o	t	t	o	n	w	o	o	d	f	x	a	t	v	r	a	g	n	h	l
d	s	z	i	a	l	n	q	w	e	t	i	u	q	s	e	m	u	l	q	e	w	o	e	i
f	t	b	v	n	v	e	l	k	p	d	c	p	a	b	f	h	o	i	n	a	e	r	u	m
w	i	a	l	y	b	t	b	r	s	v	s	o	c	o	r	n	r	m	u	o	e	d	u	w
j	c	l	i	o	z	u	n	i	a	z	j	m	c	j	b	d	t	w	n	z	p	a	o	l
l	e	a	m	n	a	v	a	h	o	d	q	a	u	s	a	a	d	l	e	v	e	p	a	m
e	a	t	w	e	e	p	a	o	k	a	e	p	y	p	r	e	e	m	g	n	q	e	o	r
p	a	m	l	c	q	e	o	g	s	l	l	c	a	a	r	a	l	r	b	k	e	a	r	a
i	x	g	b	r	e	a	r	a	c	k	a	c	u	n	a	o	k	a	e	h	a	z	a	n
c	e	u	e	e	w	e	s	n	v	m	h	t	r	i	n	z	c	n	u	l	l	i	d	d
k	g	z	w	p	h	l	b	m	o	e	s	a	s	a	c	v	e	a	t	q	u	q	l	o
p	w	h	c	z	s	e	q	r	p	s	i	e	e	r	a	n	p	e	u	v	q	m	a	m
o	h	t	l	e	a	k	e	c	v	a	v	k	m	d	s	i	s	a	l	y	l	u	a	b
c	b	e	e	n	u	a	b	t	p	i	n	t	o	s	n	w	b	o	a	q	e	x	g	a
k	s	n	i	m	q	c	e	d	n	c	b	n	e	o	r	q	m	z	l	d	u	u	o	n
e	k	c	c	g	s	d	f	k	c	o	l	f	n	l	a	l	b	v	n	o	m	t	t	a
t	i	l	g	u	b	q	g	w	q	l	p	m	v	d	g	e	o	n	w	l	c	d	u	d
u	d	e	k	z	a	n	t	e	l	o	p	e	s	a	a	a	m	k	o	o	d	g	k	j
q	p	n	l	h	o	c	v	a	e	c	i	v	e	r	c	r	e	h	i	u	i	y	t	g
h	m	s	i	l	r	e	d	t	a	i	l	e	d	h	a	w	k	s	l	r	s	g	s	e
e	f	n	h	e	m	i	s	p	h	e	r	e	k	c	l	v	q	q	y	e	z	q	k	v

NAME: ______________________

Comprehension Quiz

30

Answer each question in a complete sentence.

1. Describe 3 aspects of Bright Morning's future that she wanted. Where did she want to live? With whom? How? (3)

____

____

2. What did owning sheep mean to Bright Morning? What event in the story gives us this insight? (2)

____

____

____

3. What is the first sign of the central conflict between the Navaho and the U.S. government soldiers? (1)

____

4. Why does the author spend so much time describing the plants, animals and land formations in this novel? (1)

____

____

5. Who said: "I would rather die than go back to the village"? Why? (2)

____

____

6. Who is the hero of the story? Give 2 reasons why you have that opinion. (3)

____

____

7. What was Tall Boy's main character flaw? How did this flaw shape his actions in the story? Give 3 examples. (4)

____

____

SUBTOTAL: /16

NAME: ______________________________

Comprehension Quiz

8. Why didn't Rosita try to escape? Why did Rosita like living as a servant in the U.S. town? **2**

____

____

9. What 3 challenges or problems did Bright Morning's family face while living at Bosque Redondo? **3**

____

____

____

10. What was the significance of the baby cared for by Bright Morning during the long walk to Bosque Redondo? **1**

____

11. What is the peak or climax of the conflict in this story? **1**

____

12. What is the event that concludes the struggle or plot conflict in the novel? **2**

____

____

13. What 2 lessons did Bright Morning learn from her first capture and escape, which helped her at Bosque Redondo? **2**

____

____

____

14. What is the author's message? Defend your opinion with 2 examples from the story. **3**

____

____

____

SUBTOTAL: /14

11

1. Answers will vary.

2. Answers will vary.

Vocabulary

1. barrancas
2. mesa
3. flock
4. grove
5. corral
6. greening
7. aspen
8. pinon

12

1.

a) ✓ D

b) ✓ B

c) ✓ A

2.

a) mais/corn and peaches

b) deer

c) sheep

d) cottonwoods, aspen, pinon, (and peaches)

e) The month of the deer

13

1. She loved to see the change in nature, and she wanted to take the sheep up to the grazing land.

2. Answers will vary.

3. Bright Morning had a mother, a father and an older sister. Her older brother had died from being struck by lightning. Her friends are two girls about her age. White Deer and Running Bird, who like to tease her about her looks and her boyfriend.

4. For women, looking after the sheep was a way of proving your maturity.

5. Her mother got up and took her right back up the mountain. Her mother did not talk to her all night. Her mother did not let her take the sheep to graze all the rest of the summer.

14

1. Answers will vary.

2. Answers will vary.

Vocabulary

1. E
2. G
3. H
4. B
5. I
6. D
7. J
8. A
9. C
10. F

15

1.

a) Bright Morning's mother
b) Running Bird
c) White Deer
d) Bright Morning's sister
e) Running Bird
f) Bright Morning
g) Bright Morning's mother
h) Bright Morning
i) Running Bird
j) Bright Morning

Vocabulary

1. teased
2. proud
3. protected
4. sheep
5. raid
6. hunter
7. clan
8. obedient
9. marry
10. observant

16

1. Bright Morning's mother meets her at the gate and gives her lunch and tells her the best place for the sheep to graze.

2. Answers will vary.

3. He gave himself his name after hunting and killing a bear. He is a good hunter, he is also proud.

4. "Last summer they threatened to come back and burn our village." Running Bird said. "They are back."

5. The US soldiers were commissioned to keep the peace in the west territories. The Ute, the book says have been the enemies of the Navaho people for years.

6. If the young men were there, the soldiers may not have issued a warning because they would be obviously keeping the peace.

1. Answers will vary.

2. Answers will vary.

Vocabulary

1. E
2. H
3. I
4. B
5. G
6. A
7. F
8. C
9. D

(17)

1.

a) 2
b) 4
c) 6
d) 1
e) 5
f) 3

2.

a) ...the Spaniards approached smiling and asking for directions.

b) She realized that the Spaniards had two empty horses...

c) ...he was hit in the head and did not get up.

d) The old woman made stew out of dog meat...

e) They wanted to show that they were not going to willingly work for the slavers...

f) She gave her one look that said "Run now while you can"...

(18)

1. She was dancing because of her pride of owning so many sheep—this is foreshadowing that something bad is going to happen. Throughout the novel, when someone is too proud, they have something bring them down.

2. It was important because her mother would know that they were taken and perhaps someone from the village would come looking for them.

3. Struggle to live her life in her way. Struggle to survive as a people.

4. Bright Morning's two friends like to tease her and try to get her to talk about Tall Boy. She doesn't really tease back, she stays quiet to stop the teasing. In the end, both girls stop teasing her.

5. The girls are going to run away when the men are not watching them at night. The men tie them up so they can't move.

6. Answers will vary.

(19)

1. Answers will vary.

2. Answers will vary.

Vocabulary

Sentences will vary.

(20)

1.

a) T
b) F
c) F
d) T
e) F
f) T
g) F
h) F
i) T
j) F

2.

a) obeying
b) soldier
c) Jesu Cristos
d) Nehana

(21)

EZ✓

1. She is happy and lonely. Facts will vary.

2. She has white skin, blue eyes and hair the color of corn silk when it is ripe.

3. She thinks she is surly and she walks with pigeon toes and has a broken tooth, so she isn't as pretty as she would like for serving meals and greeting guests.

4. Answers will vary.

5. Rosita came from a bad situation and the place she's in now is better for her, but Bright Morning came from a satisfying life and the life of a slave was a worse situation for her.

6. The church is dark, with only a few candles, people are somber and crying, the image of Christ comes in with blood on his forehead, and there are whips with metal tips that people start to hit themselves with when the lights go out.

(22)

1.

The back gate was locked, there was glass on the top of the wall. She was always under the watchful eyes of Rosita.

2.

Answers will vary.

Vocabulary

1. dusk

2. lances

3. scornfully

4. crest

5. leagues

6. ridge

7. neigh

8. A draw

9. ravine

1.

a) grove

b) bit and bridle

c) stream

d) South

e) two

f) noon

g) Black Dog

h) Tall Boy

i) bow/arrow

j) rifle

k) war cry

l) medicine man

2.

a) F

b) T

c) F

d) T

e) T

1.

Answers will vary, but may include: He could have just wanted the valuable bit and bridle, or he could have wanted to capture the girls and horses.

2.

Answers will vary, but may include: Nehana didn't make it last time on her own, maybe she wanted others with her.

3.

Answers will vary, but may include: She knew that Nehana had been caught before, she also knew that Nehana could help them.

4.

The trackers' horses are fresh, and they are good riders. They also know the local area. The girls are desperate not to get captured again. They are used to hunting and being quiet and observing.

5.

Answers will vary.

6.

Answers will vary.

1.

Answers will vary.

2.

Answers will vary.

Vocabulary

1. G

2. I

3. A

4. C

5. E

6. F

7. B

8. J

9. H

10. D

1.

a) ✓ **C**

b) ✓ **D**

c) ✓ **A**

d) ✓ **A**

e) ✓ **D**

1.

Answers will vary, but may include: She really cared for him: she helped to nurse him and keep him company, she did not pity him and told him that she believed he could fully recover.

2.

She keeps her busy with work, tells her 'someone' else can make his meals, and then plans the womanhood ceremony for when he was still weak.

3.

On one hand, it appears that women have subservient roles; but in reality, many women had a lot of personal power and say in the running of the clan's daily affairs.

4.

Answers will vary.

5.

Answers will vary, but may include: He is still proud, and he doesn't want her doing things for him out of gratitude or pity.

EZ✓

EZ✓

1. Answers will vary.

2. Answers will vary.

Vocabulary

1. crevice
2. pinto beans
3. captivity
4. abandoned
5. feat
6. tethered
7. tending
8. broth
9. hatchet
10. clans

(29)

1.

a) ✓ B
b) ✓ B
c) ✓ D
d) ✓ D
e) ✓ A
f) ✓ D

(30)

1. Answers will vary.

2. Tall Boy is defiant. He still thinks that he can fight the white men and win back control of their land.

3. He realizes that his role as lead warrior and hunter has been destroyed by his injury and disability.

4. Bright Morning still treats him as a potential husband. She talks with him normally and says that she believes that he will one day be able to throw the spear as well as he used to.

5. Answers will vary, but may include: He is defiant and proud. His identity and self-worth is based on his need to be able to hunt and fight.

6. Almost all the clan names describe a geographic feature of where the clan lives.

(31)

Vocabulary

Across

1. portals
3. buzzards
5. waned
6. hides
7. quarrelsome
8. jeer
12. lame
13. fleecy
14. straggling
15. crone
16. trudged
17. idle

Down

1. prodded
2. league
3. brush
4. carrying board
6. headmen
9. ragged
10. coyote
11. falter
14. slain

(32)

1.

a) Winter

b) Little Rainbow

c) bare, bleeding, answer

d) Bright Morning's father, starving, freeze, alive

e) buzzards, died

f) cried

g) idleness, Gods, punish

(33)

1. Kindness, she just recognized the need and helped.

2. Her sister tells her she was not wise, her mother is more fatalistic: what will be will be.

3. Tall Boy is still hanging around Bright Morning, he is helping her, he cares about her AND he is starting to adjust to his disability.

4. Last Spring all was good and green and about new beginnings. This Spring is all about dark and gray and dismal.

5. Over-crowded, on the hard ground by a meandering river (which means it could flood), no good soil for farming, windy and not enough wood for fuel and construction of houses. Not enough wildlife for hunting.

6. The men could not fight, they had lost their spirit. They accepted their fate and said that the gods willed it, and they were being punished. Bright Morning scolds Tall Boy for not wanting to fight or protect his people.

(34)

1.
Answers will vary.

2.
Answers will vary.

Vocabulary

1. gourd
2. spindly
3. gruel
4. forsaken
5. scold
6. buttress
7. tend
8. waning

35

1.
a) ✓ **C**
b) ✓ **C**
c) ✓ **A**
d) ✓ **B**
e) ✓ **A**

36

1.
She starts to welcome his attention: partly because she wants the use of the horse, partly because Tall Boy has been helpful and genuinely interested in Bright Morning.

2.
Answers will vary.

3.
Her anger would not help, he would just get mad at her and stubbornly refuse to go.

4.
That is the life she wants. She is also realistic to think that they can't find everyone, and eventually they would start to die if they stayed by the fort.

5.
Answers will vary.

37

1.
Answers will vary.

2.
Answers will vary.

3.
Answers will vary.

Vocabulary

1. E
2. A
3. F
4. D
5. B
6. G
7. C

38

1.
a) horse
b) Navaho
c) six
d) Elk-Running
e) house
f) son
g) sheep
h) ewe
i) cave
j) lamb

39

1.
Gourds of flour, blankets, a knife, and sheers.

2.
Bright Morning's Mother wanted the men to fight back.

3.
Entering without asking, looking in someone's eyes, saying someone's name. If someone breaks a social law they can take offence, or make a judgment about their personality or morals.

4.
Answers will vary, but may include: It was closer, and they were running out of food.

5.
Answers will vary, but may include: She knows the value of the sheep and she is sure some have survived.

40

EZ✓

Word Search Puzzle

d	j	y	n	p	a	r	e	i	l	h	f	r	q	n	k	t	n	f	j	d	b	e	q	v
f	u	o	t	c	o	t	t	o	n	w	o	o	d	f	x	a	t	v	r	a	g	n	h	l
d	s	z	i	a	l	n	q	w	e	t	i	u	q	s	e	m	u	l	q	e	w	o	e	i
f	t	b	v	n	v	e	l	k	p	d	c	p	a	b	f	h	o	i	n	a	e	r	u	m
w	i	a	l	y	b	t	b	r	s	v	s	o	c	o	r	n	r	m	u	o	e	d	u	w
j	c	l	i	o	z	u	n	i	a	z	j	m	c	j	b	d	t	w	n	z	p	a	o	l
l	e	a	m	n	a	v	a	h	o	d	q	a	u	s	a	a	d	l	e	v	e	p	a	m
e	a	t	w	e	e	p	a	o	k	a	e	p	y	p	r	e	e	m	g	n	q	e	o	r
p	a	m	l	c	q	e	o	g	s	l	l	c	a	a	r	a	l	r	b	k	e	a	r	a
i	x	g	b	r	e	a	r	a	c	k	a	c	u	n	a	o	k	a	e	h	a	z	a	n
c	e	u	e	e	w	e	s	n	v	m	h	t	r	i	n	z	c	n	u	l	l	i	d	d
k	g	z	w	p	h	l	b	m	o	e	s	a	s	a	c	v	e	a	t	q	u	q	l	o
p	w	h	c	z	s	e	q	r	p	s	i	e	e	r	a	n	p	e	u	v	q	m	a	m
o	h	t	l	e	a	k	e	c	v	a	v	k	m	d	s	i	s	a	l	y	l	u	a	b
c	b	e	e	n	u	a	b	t	p	i	n	t	o	s	n	w	b	o	a	q	e	x	g	a
k	s	n	i	m	q	c	e	d	n	c	b	n	e	o	r	q	m	z	l	d	u	u	o	n
e	k	c	c	g	s	d	f	k	c	o	l	f	n	l	a	l	b	v	n	o	m	t	t	a
t	i	l	g	u	b	a	g	w	q	l	p	m	v	d	g	e	o	n	w	l	c	d	u	d
u	d	e	k	z	a	n	t	e	l	o	p	e	s	a	a	a	m	k	o	o	d	g	k	j
q	p	n	l	h	o	c	v	a	e	c	i	v	e	r	c	r	e	h	i	u	i	y	t	g
h	m	s	i	l	r	e	d	t	a	i	l	e	d	h	a	w	k	s	l	r	s	g	s	e
e	f	n	h	e	m	i	s	p	h	e	r	e	k	c	l	v	q	q	y	e	z	q	k	v
u	g	o	z	q	h	s	u	b	e	f	a	c	e	s	o	r	u	g	g	u	c	u	a	r
u	e	n	c	x	k	r	h	y	i	a	i	a	r	k	b	m	r	e	d	i	g	r	a	m
h	f	s	u	l	s	d	l	g	s	q	s	f	t	a	b	p	s	r	e	a	j	s	c	p

EZ✓

1. Canyon de Chelly with Tall Boy as her husband; raising her family in the Navaho culture.

2. The sheep represent her responsibility and the traditional role of the Navaho woman. During a storm, she left the sheep in the pasture, and was not allowed to care for the sheep again for a year.

3. The U.S. Army said that they would return and kill everyone in the village if the men were out raiding and not hunting.

4. The Navaho people's culture is tied to nature: their food, shelter, and spiritual beliefs are all tied to the land around them.

5. Nehana had already escaped once, and would probably be killed if she was captured again.

6. Bright Morning is the hero of the story. She plans for and succeeds in their escape and return to the Navaho lands and way of life.

7. Tall Boy was too proud. Answers will vary.

8. Her life had not been a good one, so to her the U.S. home was better than what she had in her home village.

9. Not enough food, not enough wood for heat/cooking and shelters. The Apache, Navaho and Ute were enemies. The U.S. Army and the Navaho didn't understand each other. The spread of diseases.

10. When the baby dies, it highlights why Bright Morning does not want to raise her child at Bosque Redondo.

11. The climax or peak of the conflict is when Tall Boy escapes from prison.

12. The conclusion of the conflict is when Bright Morning returns to her homeland and finds her sheep. This is the sign that she will live as a traditional Navaho wife and mother.

13. She learned that she needs a plan to escape and then take the chance and get away when you can.

14. Answers will vary.

Plot Summary

For each footprint, write a fact from the story. Start with the setting, then continue with the important event that starts the story's action. Follow this with the main events that cause the conflict to rise and reach its climax. Finally, finish off with the conclusion.

Climax

____

____

____

Rising Action

____

____

____

Falling Action

____

____

____

Introduction

____

____

____

Conclusion

____

____

____

Both Sides of the Story

There are always two sides to every story. Compare Rosita and Bright Morning's points of view about living and working for the Soldier's wife in the town. Write a quote for each person in the speech bubble. Write what each person felt in the heart. Write what each person thought in the thought bubble. In the space by each arm, write how each person acted. Finally, at the bottom, write your conclusions about the differences between each person.

Finding the Theme

Gather facts throughout the novel about the theme and write them in the circle quadrants. Remember to include the quote and page number for each fact.

Proof of theme in the plot:

Proof of theme in the character's actions:

Proof of theme in the moral or author's message:

Proof of theme in the setting, mood or atmosphere:

- **RSL.5.1** Quote accurately from a text when explaining what the text says explicitly and when drawing inferences from the text.
- **RSL.5.2** Determine a theme of a story, drama, or poem from details in the text, including how characters in a story or drama respond to challenges or how the speaker in a poem reflects upon a topic; summarize the text.
- **RSL.5.3** Compare and contrast two or more characters, settings, or events in a story or drama, drawing on specific details in the text.
- **RSL.5.4** Determine the meaning of words and phrases as they are used in a text, including figurative language such as metaphors and similes.
- **RSL.5.5** Explain how a series of chapters, scenes, or stanzas fits together to provide the overall structure of a particular story, drama, or poem.
- **RSL.5.6** Describe how a narrator's or speaker's point of view influences how events are described.
- **RSL.5.9** Compare and contrast stories in the same genre on their approaches to similar themes and topics.
- **RSL.5.10** By the end of the year read and comprehend literature, including stories, dramas, and poetry, at the high end of the grades 4–5 text complexity band independently and proficiently.
- **RSL.6.1** Cite textual evidence to support analysis of what the text says explicitly as well as inferences drawn from the text.
- **RSL.6.2** Determine a theme or central idea of a text and how it is conveyed through particular details; provide a summary of the text distinct from personal opinions or judgments.
- **RSL.6.3** Describe how a particular story's or drama's plot unfolds in a series of episodes as well as how the characters respond or change as the plot moves toward a resolution.
- **RSL.6.4** Determine the meaning of words and phrases as they are used in a text, including figurative and connotative meanings; analyze the impact of a specific word choice on meaning and tone.
- **RSL.6.5** Analyze how a particular sentence, chapter, scene, or stanza fits into the overall structure of a text and contributes to the development of the theme, setting, or plot.
- **RSL.6.6** Explain how an author develops the point of view of the narrator or speaker in a text.
- **RSL.6.10** By the end of the year read and comprehend literature, including stories, dramas, and poems, in the grades 6–8 text complexity band proficiently, with scaffolding as needed at the high end of the range.
- **RSFS.5.3** Know and apply grade-level phonics and word analysis skills in decoding words. **A)** Use combined knowledge of all letter-sound correspondences, syllabication patterns, and morphology to read accurately unfamiliar multisyllabic words in context and out of context.
- **RSFS.5.4** Read with sufficient accuracy and fluency to support comprehension. **A)** Read grade-level text with purpose and understanding. **B)** Read grade-level prose and poetry orally with accuracy, appropriate rate, and expression on successive readings. **C)** Use context to confirm or self-correct word recognition and understanding, rereading as necessary.
- **WS.5.1** Write opinion pieces on topics or texts, supporting a point of view with reasons and information. **A)** Introduce a topic or text clearly, state an opinion, and create an organizational structure in which ideas are logically grouped to support the writer's purpose. **B)** Provide logically ordered reasons that are supported by facts and details. **C)** Link opinion and reasons using words, phrases, and clauses. **D)** Provide a concluding statement or section related to the opinion presented.
- **WS.5.2** Write informative/explanatory texts to examine a topic and convey ideas and information clearly. **A)** Introduce a topic clearly, provide a general observation and focus, and group related information logically; include formatting, illustrations, and multimedia when useful to aiding comprehension. **B)** Develop the topic with facts, definitions, concrete details, quotations, or other information and examples related to the topic. **C)** Link ideas within and across categories of information using words, phrases, and clauses. **D)** Use precise language and domain-specific vocabulary to inform about or explain the topic. **E)** Provide a concluding statement or section related to the information or explanation presented.
- **WS.5.3** Write narratives to develop real or imagined experiences or events using effective technique, descriptive details, and clear event sequences. Orient the reader by establishing a situation and introducing a narrator and/or characters; organize an event sequence that unfolds naturally. **B)** Use narrative techniques, such as dialogue, description, and pacing, to develop experiences and events or show the responses of characters to situations. **C)** Use a variety of transitional words, phrases, and clauses to manage the sequence of events. **D)** Use concrete words and phrases and sensory details to convey experiences and events precisely. **E)** Provide a conclusion that follows from the narrated experiences or events.
- **WS.5.4** Produce clear and coherent writing in which the development and organization are appropriate to task, purpose, and audience.
- **WS.5.7** Conduct short research projects that use several sources to build knowledge through investigation of different aspects of a topic.
- **WS.5.8** Recall relevant information from experiences or gather relevant information from print and digital sources; summarize or paraphrase information in notes and finished work, and provide a list of sources.
- **WS.5.9** Recall relevant information from experiences or gather relevant information from print and digital sources; summarize or paraphrase information in notes and finished work, and provide a list of sources.
- **WS.6.1** Write arguments to support claims with clear reasons and relevant evidence. **A)** Introduce claim(s) and organize the reasons and evidence clearly. **B)** Support claim(s) with clear reasons and relevant evidence, using credible sources and demonstrating an understanding of the topic or text. **C)** Use words, phrases, and clauses to clarify the relationships among claim(s) and reasons. **D)** Establish and maintain a formal style. **E)** Provide a concluding statement or section that follows from the argument presented.
- **WS.6.2** Write informative/explanatory texts to examine a topic and convey ideas, concepts, and information through the selection, organization, and analysis of relevant content. **A)** Introduce a topic; organize ideas, concepts, and information, using strategies such as definition, classification, comparison/contrast, and cause/effect; include formatting, graphics, and multimedia when useful to aiding comprehension. **B)** Develop the topic with relevant facts, definitions, concrete details, quotations, or other information and examples. **C)** Use appropriate transitions to clarify the relationships among ideas and concepts. **D)** Use precise language and domain-specific vocabulary to inform about or explain the topic. **E)** Establish and maintain a formal style. **F)** Provide a concluding statement or section that follows from the information or explanation presented.
- **WS.6.3** Write narratives to develop real or imagined experiences or events using effective technique, relevant descriptive details, and well-structured event sequences. **A)** Engage and orient the reader by establishing a context and introducing a narrator and/or characters; organize an event sequence that unfolds naturally and logically. **B)** Use narrative techniques, such as dialogue, pacing, and description, to develop experiences, events, and/or characters. **C)** Use a variety of transition words, phrases, and clauses to convey sequence and signal shifts from one time frame or setting to another. **D)** Use precise words and phrases, relevant descriptive details, and sensory language to convey experiences and events. **E)** Provide a conclusion that follows from the narrated experiences or events.
- **WS.6.4** Produce clear and coherent writing in which the development, organization, and style are appropriate to task, purpose, and audience.
- **WS.6.7** Conduct short research projects to answer a question, drawing on several sources and refocusing the inquiry when appropriate.
- **WS.6.8** Gather relevant information from multiple print and digital sources; assess the credibility of each source; and quote or paraphrase the data and conclusions of others while avoiding plagiarism and providing basic bibliographic information for sources.
- **WS.6.9** Draw evidence from literary or informational texts to support analysis, reflection, and research. **A)** Apply *grade 6 Reading standards* to literature. **B)** Apply *grade 6 Reading standards* to literary nonfiction.

Publication Listing

Ask Your Dealer About Our Complete Line

SOCIAL STUDIES - Software

ITEM #	TITLE
	MAPPING SKILLS SERIES
CC7770	Grades PK-2 Mapping Skills with Google Earth
CC7771	Grades 3-5 Mapping Skills with Google Earth
CC7772	Grades 6-8 Mapping Skills with Google Earth
CC7773	Grades PK-8 Mapping Skills with Google Earth Big Box

SOCIAL STUDIES - Books

	MAPPING SKILLS SERIES
CC5786	Grades PK-2 Mapping Skills with Google Earth
CC5787	Grades 3-5 Mapping Skills with Google Earth
CC5788	Grades 6-8 Mapping Skills with Google Earth
CC5789	Grades PK-8 Mapping Skills with Google Earth Big Book
	NORTH AMERICAN GOVERNMENTS SERIES
CC5757	American Government
CC5758	Canadian Government
CC5759	Mexican Government
CC5760	Governments of North America Big Book
	WORLD GOVERNMENTS SERIES
CC5761	World Political Leaders
CC5762	World Electoral Processes
CC5763	Capitalism vs. Communism
CC5777	World Politics Big Book
	WORLD CONFLICT SERIES
CC5511	American Revolutionary War
CC5500	American Civil War
CC5512	American Wars Big Book
CC5501	World War I
CC5502	World War II
CC5503	World Wars I & II Big Book
CC5505	Korean War
CC5506	Vietnam War
CC5507	Korean & Vietnam Wars Big Book
CC5508	Persian Gulf War (1990-1991)
CC5509	Iraq War (2003-2010)
CC5510	Gulf Wars Big Book
	WORLD CONTINENTS SERIES
CC5750	North America
CC5751	South America
CC5768	The Americas Big Book
CC5752	Europe
CC5753	Africa
CC5754	Asia
CC5755	Australia
CC5756	Antarctica
	WORLD CONNECTIONS SERIES
CC5782	Culture, Society & Globalization
CC5783	Economy & Globalization
CC5784	Technology & Globalization
CC5785	Globalization Big Book

REGULAR & REMEDIAL EDUCATION

Reading Level 3-4 Grades 5-8

ENVIRONMENTAL STUDIES - Software

ITEM #	TITLE
	CLIMATE CHANGE SERIES
CC7747	Global Warming: Causes Grades 3-8
CC7748	Global Warming: Effects Grades 3-8
CC7749	Global Warming: Reduction Grades 3-8
CC7750	Global Warming Big Box Grades 3-8

ENVIRONMENTAL STUDIES - Books

	MANAGING OUR WASTE SERIES
CC5764	Waste: At the Source
CC5765	Prevention, Recycling & Conservation
CC5766	Waste: The Global View
CC5767	Waste Management Big Book
	CLIMATE CHANGE SERIES
CC5769	Global Warming: Causes
CC5770	Global Warming: Effects
CC5771	Global Warming: Reduction
CC5772	Global Warming Big Book
	GLOBAL WATER SERIES
CC5773	Conservation: Fresh Water Resources
CC5774	Conservation: Ocean Water Resources
CC5775	Conservation: Waterway Habitat Resources
CC5776	Water Conservation Big Book
	CARBON FOOTPRINT SERIES
CC5778	Reducing Your Own Carbon Footprint
CC5779	Reducing Your School's Carbon Footprint
CC5780	Reducing Your Community's Carbon Footprint
CC5781	Carbon Footprint Big Book

SCIENCE - Software

ITEM #	TITLE
	SPACE AND BEYOND SERIES
CC7557	Solar System Grades 5-8
CC7558	Galaxies & the Universe Grades 5-8
CC7559	Space Travel & Technology Grades 5-8
CC7560	Space Big Box Grades 5-8
	HUMAN BODY SERIES
CC7549	Cells, Skeletal & Muscular Systems Grades 5-8
CC7550	Senses, Nervous & Respiratory Systems Grades 5-8
CC7551	Circulatory, Digestive & Reproductive Systems Grades 5-8
CC7552	Human Body Big Box Grades 5-8
	FORCE, MOTION & SIMPLE MACHINES SERIES
CC7553	Force Grades 3-8
CC7554	Motion Grades 3-8
CC7555	Simple Machines Grades 3-8
CC7556	Force, Motion & Simple Machines Big Box Grades 3-8

SCIENCE - Books

	ECOLOGY & THE ENVIRONMENT SERIES
CC4500	Ecosystems
CC4501	Classification & Adaptation
CC4502	Cells
CC4503	Ecology & The Environment Big Book
	MATTER & ENERGY SERIES
CC4504	Properties of Matter
CC4505	Atoms, Molecules & Elements
CC4506	Energy
CC4507	The Nature of Matter Big Book
	FORCE & MOTION SERIES
CC4508	Force
CC4509	Motion
CC4510	Simple Machines
CC4511	Force, Motion & Simple Machines Big Book
	SPACE & BEYOND SERIES
CC4512	Solar System
CC4513	Galaxies & The Universe
CC4514	Travel & Technology
CC4515	Space Big Book
	HUMAN BODY SERIES
CC4516	Cells, Skeletal & Muscular Systems
CC4517	Senses, Nervous & Respiratory Systems
CC4518	Circulatory, Digestive & Reproductive Systems
CC4519	Human Body Big Book

VISIT:
www.CLASSROOM COMPLETE PRESS.com
To view sample pages from each book

LITERATURE KITS™ - Books

ITEM #	TITLE
	GRADES 1-2
CC2100	Curious George (H. A. Rey)
CC2101	Paper Bag Princess (Robert N. Munsch)
CC2102	Stone Soup (Marcia Brown)
CC2103	The Very Hungry Caterpillar (Eric Carle)
CC2104	Where the Wild Things Are (Maurice Sendak)
	GRADES 3-4
CC2300	Babe: The Gallant Pig (Dick King-Smith)
CC2301	Because of Winn-Dixie (Kate DiCamillo)
CC2302	The Tale of Despereaux (Kate DiCamillo)
CC2303	James and the Giant Peach (Roald Dahl)
CC2304	Ramona Quimby, Age 8 (Beverly Cleary)
CC2305	The Mouse and the Motorcycle (Beverly Cleary)
CC2306	Charlotte's Web (E.B. White)
CC2307	Owls in the Family (Farley Mowat)
CC2308	Sarah, Plain and Tall (Patricia MacLachlan)
CC2309	Matilda (Roald Dahl)
CC2310	Charlie & The Chocolate Factory (Roald Dahl)
CC2311	Frindle (Andrew Clements)
CC2312	M.C. Higgins, the Great (Virginia Hamilton)
CC2313	The Family Under The Bridge (N.S. Carlson)
CC2314	The Hundred Penny Box (Sharon Mathis)
CC2315	Cricket in Times Square (George Selden)
CC2316	Fantastic Mr Fox (Roald Dahl)
CC2317	The Hundred Dresses (Eleanor Estes)
	GRADES 5-6
CC2500	Black Beauty (Anna Sewell)
CC2501	Bridge to Terabithia (Katherine Paterson)
CC2502	Bud, Not Buddy (Christopher Paul Curtis)
CC2503	The Egypt Game (Zilpha Keatley Snyder)
CC2504	The Great Gilly Hopkins (Katherine Paterson)
CC2505	Holes (Louis Sachar)
CC2506	Number the Stars (Lois Lowry)
CC2507	The Sign of the Beaver (E.G. Speare)
CC2508	The Whipping Boy (Sid Fleischman)
CC2509	Island of the Blue Dolphins (Scott O'Dell)
CC2510	Underground to Canada (Barbara Smucker)
CC2511	Loser (Jerry Spinelli)
CC2512	The Higher Power of Lucky (Susan Patron)
CC2513	Kira-Kira (Cynthia Kadohata)
CC2514	Dear Mr. Henshaw (Beverly Cleary)
CC2515	The Summer of the Swans (Betsy Byars)
CC2516	Shiloh (Phyllis Reynolds Naylor)
CC2517	A Single Shard (Linda Sue Park)
CC2518	Hoot (Carl Hiaasen)
CC2519	Hatchet (Gary Paulsen)
CC2520	The Giver (Lois Lowry)
CC2521	The Graveyard Book (Neil Gaiman)
CC2522	The View From Saturday (E.L. Konigsburg)
CC2523	Hattie Big Sky (Kirby Larson)
CC2524	When You Reach Me (Rebecca Stead)
CC2525	Criss Cross (Lynne Rae Perkins)
CC2526	A Year Down Yonder (Richard Peck)
CC2527	Maniac Magee (Jerry Spinelli)

LITERATURE KITS™ - Books

ITEM #	TITLE
CC2528	From the Mixed-Up Files of Mrs. Basil E. Frankweiler (E.L. Konigsburg)
CC2529	Sing Down the Moon (Scott O'Dell)
	GRADES 7-8
CC2700	Cheaper by the Dozen (Frank B. Gilbreth)
CC2701	The Miracle Worker (William Gibson)
CC2702	The Red Pony (John Steinbeck)
CC2703	Treasure Island (Robert Louis Stevenson)
CC2704	Romeo & Juliet (William Shakespeare)
CC2705	Crispin: The Cross of Lead (Avi)
CC2707	The Boy in the Striped Pajamas (John Boyne)
CC2708	The Westing Game (Ellen Raskin)
	GRADES 9-12
CC2001	To Kill A Mockingbird (Harper Lee)
CC2002	Angela's Ashes (Frank McCourt)
CC2003	The Grapes of Wrath (John Steinbeck)
CC2004	The Good Earth (Pearl S. Buck)
CC2005	The Road (Cormac McCarthy)
CC2006	The Old Man and the Sea (Ernest Hemingway)
CC2007	Lord of the Flies (William Golding)
CC2008	The Color Purple (Alice Walker)
CC2009	The Outsiders (S.E. Hinton)
CC2010	Hamlet (William Shakespeare)
CC2012	The Adventures of Huckleberry Finn (Mark Twain)
CC2013	Macbeth (William Shakespeare)

LANGUAGE ARTS - Software

CC7112	**Word Families - Short Vowels** Grades PK-2
CC7113	**Word Families - Long Vowels** Grades PK-2
CC7114	**Word Families - Vowels Big Box** Grades PK-2
CC7100	**High Frequency Sight Words** Grades PK-2
CC7101	**High Frequency Picture Words** Grades PK-2
CC7102	**Sight & Picture Words Big Box** Grades PK-2
CC7104	**How to Write a Paragraph** Grades 3-8
CC7105	**How to Write a Book Report** Grades 3-8
CC7106	**How to Write an Essay** Grades 3-8
CC7107	**Master Writing Big Box** Grades 3-8
CC7108	**Reading Comprehension** Grades 5-8
CC7109	**Literary Devices** Grades 5-8
CC7110	**Critical Thinking** Grades 5-8
CC7111	**Master Reading Big Box** Grades 5-8

LANGUAGE ARTS - Books

CC1110	Word Families - Short Vowels Grades K-1
CC1111	Word Families - Long Vowels Grades K-1
CC1112	Word Families - Vowels Big Book Grades K-1
CC1113	High Frequency Sight Words Grades K-1
CC1114	High Frequency Picture Words Grades K-1
CC1115	Sight & Picture Words Big Book Grades K-1
CC1100	How to Write a Paragraph Grades 5-8
CC1101	How to Write a Book Report Grades 5-8
CC1102	How to Write an Essay Grades 5-8
CC1103	Master Writing Big Book Grades 5-8
CC1116	**Reading Comprehension** Grades 5-8
CC1117	**Literary Devices** Grades 5-8
CC1118	**Critical Thinking** Grades 5-8
CC1119	**Master Reading Big Book** Grades 5-8
CC1106	Reading Response Forms: Grades 1-2
CC1107	Reading Response Forms: Grades 3-4
CC1108	Reading Response Forms: Grades 5-6
CC1109	Reading Response Forms Big Book: Grades 1-6

MATHEMATICS - Software

ITEM #	TITLE
	PRINCIPLES & STANDARDS OF MATH SERIES
CC7315	Grades PK-2 Five Strands of Math Big Box
CC7316	Grades 3-5 Five Strands of Math Big Box
CC7317	Grades 6-8 Five Strands of Math Big Box

MATHEMATICS - Books

	TASK SHEETS
CC3100	Grades PK-2 Number & Operations Task Sheets
CC3101	Grades PK-2 Algebra Task Sheets
CC3102	Grades PK-2 Geometry Task Sheets
CC3103	Grades PK-2 Measurement Task Sheets
CC3104	Grades PK-2 Data Analysis & Probability Task Sheets
CC3105	Grades PK-2 Five Strands of Math Big Book Task Sheets
CC3106	Grades 3-5 Number & Operations Task Sheets
CC3107	Grades 3-5 Algebra Task Sheets
CC3108	Grades 3-5 Geometry Task Sheets
CC3109	Grades 3-5 Measurement Task Sheets
CC3110	Grades 3-5 Data Analysis & Probability Task Sheets
CC3111	Grades 3-5 Five Strands of Math Big Book Task Sheets
CC3112	Grades 6-8 Number & Operations Task Sheets
CC3113	Grades 6-8 Algebra Task Sheets
CC3114	Grades 6-8 Geometry Task Sheets
CC3115	Grades 6-8 Measurement Task Sheets
CC3116	Grades 6-8 Data Analysis & Probability Task Sheets
CC3117	Grades 6-8 Five Strands of Math Big Book Task Sheets
	DRILL SHEETS
CC3200	Grades PK-2 Number & Operations Drill Sheets
CC3201	Grades PK-2 Algebra Drill Sheets
CC3202	Grades PK-2 Geometry Drill Sheets
CC3203	Grades PK-2 Measurement Drill Sheets
CC3204	Grades PK-2 Data Analysis & Probability Drill Sheets
CC3205	Grades PK-2 Five Strands of Math Big Book Drill Sheets
CC3206	Grades 3-5 Number & Operations Drill Sheets
CC3207	Grades 3-5 Algebra Drill Sheets
CC3208	Grades 3-5 Geometry Drill Sheets
CC3209	Grades 3-5 Measurement Drill Sheets
CC3210	Grades 3-5 Data Analysis & Probability Drill Sheets
CC3211	Grades 3-5 Five Strands of Math Big Book Drill Sheets
CC3212	Grades 6-8 Number & Operations Drill Sheets
CC3213	Grades 6-8 Algebra Drill Sheets
CC3214	Grades 6-8 Geometry Drill Sheets
CC3215	Grades 6-8 Measurement Drill Sheets
CC3216	Grades 6-8 Data Analysis & Probability Drill Sheets
CC3217	Grades 6-8 Five Strands of Math Big Book Drill Sheets
	TASK & DRILL SHEETS
CC3300	Grades PK-2 Number & Operations Task & Drill Sheets
CC3301	Grades PK-2 Algebra Task & Drill Sheets
CC3302	Grades PK-2 Geometry Task & Drill Sheets
CC3303	Grades PK-2 Measurement Task & Drill Sheets
CC3304	Grades PK-2 Data Analysis & Probability Task & Drills
CC3306	Grades 3-5 Number & Operations Task & Drill Sheets
CC3307	Grades 3-5 Algebra Task & Drill Sheets
CC3308	Grades 3-5 Geometry Task & Drill Sheets
CC3309	Grades 3-5 Measurement Task & Drill Sheets
CC3310	Grades 3-5 Data Analysis & Probability Task & Drills
CC3312	Grades 6-8 Number & Operations Task & Drill Sheets
CC3313	Grades 6-8 Algebra Task & Drill Sheets
CC3314	Grades 6-8 Geometry Task & Drill Sheets
CC3315	Grades 6-8 Measurement Task & Drill Sheets
CC3316	Grades 6-8 Data Analysis & Probability Task & Drills